T0374029

Poems from the Heart

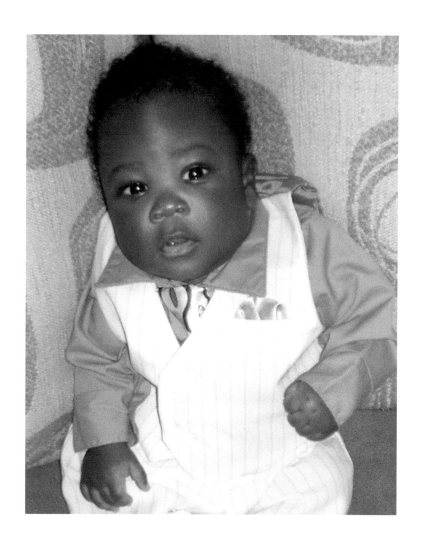

T.J. Mondesir

To order additional copies of this book, contact:
Xlibris
844-714-8691
www.Xlibris.com
Orders@Xlibris.com

ISBN: Softcover   978-1-4257-8711-0
            Hardcover   978-1-4363-1343-8

Print information available on the last page

Rev. date: 05/22/2025

Poems from the heart

Thanks to my Lord, family, friends and especially to Shirlin Merisier for being my inspiration to write my first poetry book. Love always. This book was written ten years ago, however, this is the season that the Lord had blessed me to express my voice to the world.

Thank you to the following people for allowing me to add their picture in my first poetry book.

To My Sweet nephew and He goes with me
Tyrese Dubuisson
Tyler Dubuisson
Trevon Dubuisson
Treshawn Dubuisson
Elijah Nathan Jean-Baptiste
Eddy Jean-Baptiste jr.
Eric Marcus Jean-Baptiste

My sister and Marriage could be
Nehemi Pierre Jean-Baptiste
Naomi Pierre Dubuisson
Eddy Jean-Baptiste
Jean Dubuisson

Around I go
Jeremiah

The sky is the limit and A friend
Parshall Seraphin
Toddrick Harris

I wish upon a star
Sheila Juste Dieuveille
Reynold Dieuveille
Genesis Lopez-Gonzalez
Devin Talley

This pretty girl and A friend
Jasmine Overby

My love
Susan Morgan
Lily Mondesir
Isabella J. Ramsey

A Baby love
Kiana Gonzalez
Tyrese Dubuisson

Good night talk to you tomorrow
Jeilah McKenzie Harris-Seraphin

A friend
Jacquelyn Pinaund

A Mother love
Ruth Juste

What I want to be
T.J. Mondesir

Table of contents

Joy

He goes with me...

He goes with me to the mill.
He goes with me to the hill.
He goes with me wherever my heart goes.

He goes with me as the wind blow.
He goes with me as I go low.
He goes with me wherever my heart goes.

He goes with me as high as the sky.
He goes with me as far as I can fly.
He goes with me wherever my heart goes.

He goes with me to be free.
He goes with me to be ease.
He goes with me wherever my heart goes.

He goes with me to be one.
He goes with me to be love.

To my sweet nephew

Tyler

Trevon

Eric

Tyrese

Eddy

Treshawn

Elijah

To my sweet nephew
I loved you from the first time it
was announced that you were growing within your mother womb.

To my sweet nephew
I could not wait for that day to see you born
so I can hold the gift that was sent from heaven.

To my sweet nephew
I was filled with joy when
I saw that moment has arrived for you to enter this world.
My heart was beating out of control as happiness filled it so.
I knew the Lord had blessed me with a beautiful baby I can
Call him my nephew.

To my sweet nephew
I love you so much it makes
My heart filled with excitement because I'm becoming a new aunt.

To my sweet nephew
I pray the Lord will
Always be with you wherever you may go.

To my sweet nephew
I pray that the
Lord will protect you from all dangers.

To my sweet nephew
I pray that the Lord
Will use you to
Deliver the good
News wherever…you may go

I love you my sweet nephew…

A baby love

A baby love is the way it looks at you
With love in its eyes.

A baby love is the way it smiles
As you enter the room with love in its eyes.

A baby love is the way it looks for you
When it cries for its comfort.

A baby love is the way it makes you
Smiles no matter how you feel.

A sister love

A sister love can be a special bond
That cannot be broken.

A sister love can be a shoulder you
Can cry on when times are bad.

A sister love can be a strength you
Need to push you along the way.

A sister love can be a friend
You can talk to anytime of the day.

A sister love can be like
A precious diamond that will
Always be bright like a rainbow.

A sister love is always there through
All your heavenly and devilish ways
She will always love you because
You are her sister.

Around I go

Around, around and around I go.

Around I go fast like a horse as I go
Around and around for you.

Around, around and around I go.

Around I go slowly like a turtle as I go
Around and round for you.

Around, around and around I go.

Around I go flying like a bird as I go
Around and around for your love.

Around, around and around I go...
I go around to
Be with you.

The sky is the limit

The sky is the limit…where dreams
Of true soul mate come true.

The sky is the limit…where dreams
Of true happiness do come true.

The sky is the limit…where dreams
Of true freedom to love do come true.

The sky is the limit…where dreams do come true.

Believe in yourself.

Believe in yourself that you are special.

Believe in yourself that you are loved.

Believe in yourself that you can do it.

Believe in yourself that all doors of
Opportunity is opening for you

Believe in yourself and your dreams will come true.

Love

Love is loving me for who I am.

Love is enjoying my company.

Love is missing me when I am not there.

Love is respecting me.

Love is believing in me.

Love is caring when I am hurt.

Love is forgiving me of my mistakes.

Love is holding me in your arms to protect me.

Love is saying I love you.

Jesus Love

Jesus love is wonderful like a parent bringing new life into this world.

Jesus love is great like a victorious is to his enemies.

Jesus love is fulfilling like a desire to a dream coming true.

Jesus love is power like a leader is to his followers.

Jesus love is loved like a spouse, friend, parent and sibling is to you.

My love

My love is delicate like a flower as it bloom
To give you all the decoration your heart desires.

My love is rosy like a rose as it brighten
You up to give you all the joy your heart desires.

My love is fulfilling like a sunflower as it blossom
To give you all the food your heart desires.

My love is pure like a lily as it lighten
You up to give you all your heart desires.

My love is a vase filled with different flower
As it give you love and happiness to love
Me forever…

Joy

You are my joy...because you are the source to my happiness.

You are my joy...because you are the sun that brightens up my day.

You are my joy
Because you are the provider that
Provide me with all the things I need.

You are my joy
Because you are the protector that
Protect me from dangers.

You are my joy...because you are the savior that saves me...from all my sins.

You are my joy...because you are my life and the strength of my joy.

Epiphany

I have no idea to give to you today...

I have no idea to give to you today
For the day is long with no moon to end the day.

I have no idea to give to you today
For the day is dark with no sun to shine the day.

I have no idea to give to you today
For the grass is dry with no tear to rain the day.

I have no idea to give to you today
For the flower is leaning with no stem to hold it up for the day.

I have no idea to give to you today
For I have no clue for the day.

I used to love him

I used to love him like a bear loves his fur.

I used to love him like a cat loves his prey.

I used to love him like an owl loves his stray.

I used to love him like a lion loves his steal.

I used to love him yesterday as do I love him today.

I want to be a Christian

To find peace and strength to help me through my
Darkest and brightest days…
To be a solider in the army of the Lord.
To be a dweller in the house of the Lord as he dwells in me.

I want to be a singer
To sing with joy, happiness as an angel
Reaching out to touch the heart of souls to
Find harmony in this world that is filled with hatred.

I want to be a movie star
To be the light … to show the world what
The Lord hands can do as he turns dreams to reality.
To be his eyes, arms, and legs to walk with the riches, but
Always putting God first as he lead me to bring even the richest
Person to dwell in his house.

I want to be a writer
To write the words of wisdom and to brighten
Or lift a person soul.
To give hope that the Lord lives.
To give inspiration to others that love live within
And to build a better place for my and your children.

I want to be a good wife
To be an example to others that
The evil one cannot broke the house the
Lord had built.
To be a counselor to tell others no
Matter the storms the Lord will touch
And heal where we will now
Know the hands of our Lord.

I want to be a good mother
To give knowledge, courage and drive
To tell my children that they can be anything if they just believe.
To teach my children putting God first will help
Them throughout their thunder, tornado, and rainy days.
That the sun will come out and dry the tears of pain away as
The rainbow will be their guide to shine with different colors
To lead them home.
I want to be loved for I am.

I Am Scared

I am scared because who am I?

I am scared because what will I become?

I am scared where am I going?

I am scared because will I be loved?

I am scared...

Fear

Who are you?

Who are you for me to be afraid of you?

Who are you for me to run when you are near?

Who are you that make my heart pace when trouble comes my way?

Who are you that make me cry when I cannot win?

Who are you to tell me I cannot be that Extraordinary person I was born to be?

Who are you?

I AM FEAR

You laugh

You laugh when I say I have a dream.

You laugh when I say I have a dream to be a writer.

You laugh when I say I have a dream to be an actress.

You laugh when I say I have a dream to be successful.

You just keep on laughing because I have a dream.

My name has change

My name has changed to superior
Because I have overcome my failure in life.

My name has changed to love
Because I can forgive and love my enemies.

My name has changed to witty
Because I can make you laugh when
You are sad.

My name has changed to trustworthy
Because I can be trusted when I say
I will be there.

My name has changed to outgoing
Because I can go as far as my mind
Will allow me to go.

My name has changed to outspoken
Because I can speak what's on my mind.

My name has changed to someone special
Because I am me.

My brother love

My brother love is there to protect me.

My brother love is there to tell
Me when I am wrong.

My brother love is there to help
Me along the way.

My brother love is there through my
Good and rough times.

My brother love is there to help me to
Elevate my goals.

My brother love is always there for me
Because he is my brother.

Free

I want to be free of my fears
That I may not be loved

I want to be free of my angers
That I may not succeed

I want to be free of my guilt's
That the world my not see
My gift to write

I want to be free of my sins
That I may not be forgiven for all the
Wrong doing I have done

I want to be free like a bird
That I may spread my wings to fly
As my readers know me as one who
Have a voice to express my opinions to the world.

I am free.

Emotion

This pretty Girl...

This pretty girl with no face to call her own...

This pretty girl with no face to call her own as
Paint on her eyebrows to find herself.

This girl with no face to call her own as
Paint on her eyelashes to find herself.

This girl with no face to call her own as
Paint on her eyeliner under her eyes to find herself.

This girl with no face to call her own as
Paint on her rouge to find herself.

But

This pretty girl with no face to call her own
Does not know she is beautiful just being herself.

By her intelligence
By her grace
By her walk
By her style
By her smile
By her inner beauty.

This pretty girl with no face to call her own just
Need to be herself ...by being elegant with-in to find a
Face she can call her own...

To that boy

To that boy...oh, what you may call it
Just sits there to watch my every move.

To that boy...oh, what you may call it
Just sits there to watch me when I am
Down and vulnerable.

To that boy...oh, what you may call it
Just sits there to watch me when he
Just made his move in.

To that boy...oh, what you may call it
Just sits there to watch me when he
Can abuse me.

To that boy...oh, what you may call it
Just sits there to watch me when he
Takes advantage of my broken heart.

To that boy...oh, what you may call it
Just sits there to watch me when I
Start to react.

To that boy... oh, what you may call it
Just sits there to watch me when I
Walk out of his abusive life.

To that boy...oh, what you may call it
Just sits there and ponder
How I could do that...

To that boy... what you may call it
I just can and I did!

I just want to be loved...

I just want to be loved
Not to be treated like a box
Filled with hard candy that cannot
Be broken easily.

I just want to be loved
Not to be craved for when I am needed
Or when the taste of desire is gone...
To be thrown away as
A pain to a tooth.

I just want to be loved
Not to be pick up again as the
Craving returns for the pleasure of the moment.
Not to be eaten for the flavor of joy or to save my feeling...
Like I have no choice
But
To allow myself to be eaten again... just because I want to be
Loved...no matter how the love may come.

I just want to be loved
Not to allow myself to be treated like a hard candy.

I just want to be loved...not knowing I am not a hard candy. I have feeling and can break into million pieces.

I just want to be loved...for who I am.

I just want to be loved...not for the things I can do or have.

I just want to be loved... Not to be abuse
Not to be used
Not to be amuse for enjoyment.
But

I just want to be loved for me!

Who do you think you are?

Who do you think you are?
By judging me of my mistakes.

Who do you think you are?
By telling me I am not good for society.

Who do you think you are?
By giving me a name that can only be you…

Who do you think you are?
By thinking that you are better than me in
Everything I do.

Who do you think you are?
By looking down on me as I was nothing
But a use doll…that someone has thrown away in a trash.

Who do you think you are?

You cannot judge me!
You cannot tell me I am an outcast to society.
You cannot call me any kind of names.
You cannot say you are better than me.
You cannot look down on me as a use doll…
For you are not better than me
For you are me!

I wish upon a star

I wish upon a star that the world has been at peace.

I wish upon a star that the war has been ended.

I wish upon a star that the hungry has been feed.

I wish upon a star that the poor has been clothed

I wish upon a star that the sick has been healed

And

I wish upon a star that the children have been safe from harm.

I wish upon a star that there's no more pain
And
Suffering on the earth.

I wish upon the star that the world has become
One with harmony.

I just wished upon a star.

Where were you father when I needed your love?

Where were you father when I needed a father?

Where were you when I needed a father shoulders to cry on?

Where were you when I needed a father when I was in trouble?

Where were you when I needed help with dating?

Where were you when I needed a father to say that is my child?

Where were you when I needed a father helping hand alone the way?

Where were you when I needed a father to give me a hug
And say I love you?

Where were you when I needed to say I love you daddy?

Where are you dad?

I did not mean to love you too much...

I did not mean to love you too much…
I just wanted to love you
Not steal your love away
From your mother.

I did not mean to love you too much…
I just wanted to love you
Not to make you into my child.

I did not mean to love you too much…
I just wanted to love you
Not make everyone think I'm your mother.

I did not mean to love you too much…
I just wanted to love you
Not to make your mother feel
Insecure about your love.

I did not mean to love you too much…
I just wanted to love you
Because you are the image of me.
I did not mean to love too much, but I do.

A lost Dream

I had a dream you was mine from
The first time I lay my eyes on you.

I had a dream you and I become one.

I had a dream you was my friend and lover.

I had a dream you was my husband.

I had a dream you was the father to my kids.

But
I lost the dream when I lost myself
To a sinful fuddle of temptation
Now
I have no one to blame for my lost dreams…
You will always be a dream that was
Never mine

My lost dream.

Don't give me the run around

Don't give me the run around…
Just say what's on your mind.

Don't give me the run around…
Just say what's in your heart.
Do you love me?
Do you want me?

Don't give me the run around…
When you see me with someone else you become
jealous
Giving me the mix signal.

Don't give me the run around…
When you see I enter a room you act nervous
With a smile on your face
Giving me the mix signal.

Don't give me the run around…
When you see me you cannot look into my eyes
without
Blushing
Giving me the mix signal.

Don't give me the run around…
When I think you care…you just get up
And leave out of my life
Giving me the mix signal.

Don't give me the run around…
Because I do not have time to run around
Receiving any mix signals.

Separate

Separate can be defined into different meanings.

Separate can be death.

Separate can be divorce.

Separate can be leaving a friend because of it evil ways.

Separate can be breaking up from a relationship with God.

Separate can be leaving your favorite places, things, people, food and activities.

Separate is hard to do, but separate can be an open door for a better life.

No More Pain

As I feel no more pain from my lover's abusive ways…
I climb the ladder from low self-esteem…and lift up my head in pride.
No more pain I cried….
As I feel no more pain from my lover's fists for days…
I build a wall to hide my soul of pain…to carry on my ride.
No more pain I cried…
I balled all my fears in my hand…to ball my fist up…
to give a mighty blow.
As I feel no more pain, punching down all closed doors…from my lover's
revulsion against me…in pain. I cried out… no more pain. As I no longer feel low…
As I rise in anger of my lover's vain.
No more pain I cried….
As I gain control of my will to live in peace, harmony and love …
As I gain all of me from my lover's fists of pain…I find me…
As I gain all of my pure dove…
As I stand strong like a tree…no wind cannot blow…I gain the will to
To control the fists…and no more pain I cried…

Don't cry my sweet baby

Don't cry my sweet baby mommy is here
To comfort your needs.

Don't cry my sweet baby mommy is here
To give you all the loving you need.

Don't cry my sweet baby mommy is here
To protect your loving heart.

Don't cry my sweet baby mommy is here
To love you because you
Are my sweetest baby.

Don't cry.

Marriage should be...

Marriage should be about love because it's one.

Marriage should be about trust because it's commitment.

Marriage should be about respect because it's consideration.

Marriage should be about faith because it's hopeful.

Marriage should be God first because it's a blessed reunion.

A friend

A friend is a person who loves you.

A friend is a person who understands you.

A friend is a person who supports you.
throughout
Your good and bad times.

A friend is a person who you can confide.
And can talk to in the middle of the night.

A friend is a person who can keep all your secrets.

A friend is a person who will never leave you
If you have no money.

A friend is a person who will always love you and help you to
Become a better person.

Money

Money can pay all your bills
As you are debts free.

Money can buy you fancy clothes
As you are on a shopping spree.

Money can buy you a closet full of shoes in all colors and styles
for each occasion as you are dancing with me.

Money can buy you tickets to travel across the world
As you can see.

Money can buy you a nice big house
As you plant a big tree.

Money can buy you a lot of friends
As you party with we.

Money can give you power
As you are there.

But
Money cannot buy you true love
For you are used.

Money cannot buy true friends
For you are abused.

Money cannot give you true happiness.
For you are confused.

Money cannot make a house into a home.
For you are not amused.

However
Money can take your life if
You abuse it the wrong way.

Trust

Trust is believing in me.

Trust is depending on me being there.

Trust is knowing me.

Trust is respecting me.

Trust is honoring me.

Why leave…

Why leave when times are bad?
With no hope to dream.

Why leave when times are getting tougher?
With no rain to cry.

Why leave when you know I have no one to support me?
With no sun to brighten up the day.

Why leave when you know my money is gone?
With no water to make the flower grow.

Why leave when you know I am having your second child?
With no glue to hold the future.

Why leave me?
Why leave your child?
Why leave your unborn child?
With no limbs to walk.

As you did leave…

Hold me

Hold me when I am happy… to jump
with joy for you.

Hold me when I need your help…to give
me courage to succeed.

Hold me when I am ill…to give me the
healing my soul need.

Hold me when I am afraid…to give me
peace of mind.

Hold me when I feel blue…to give me
strength to find.

Hold me when I need your loving …to
give me security to be

Hold me when I feel alone…to give me
the comfort I dear.
Just hold me near.

It hurts

It hurts when you degrade me.

It hurts when you disown me in front of your
friends.

It hurts when you show me that you are a
hypocrite.

It hurts when you dishonor me.

It hurts when you control me in everything I do.

It hurts when you say I love you and turn
around and beat me.

It hurts when you say I will never be anything
With-out you.

It hurts when you do not support me.

It hurts when you do not believe in me

It hurts when you do not care when I am ill.

It hurts when you do not hold me when I cry.

It hurts when you do everything to hold me
down
From succeeding
It hurts…

A mother love

A mother love is like
A hot cocoa that will keep
Your body warm.

A mother love is like
A sun that will keep you bright as a
Colorful rainbow.

A mother love is like
A garden of flowers that will blossom
Your days.

A mother love is like
A book that will give you all the
Information you need about life.

A mother love is like
A bull dog that will protect you from
Dangers and enemies.

A mother love is like
Your best friend…. because
She loves you.

Death

I Run

I run when you call out my name.

I run when you try to pin me down.

I run when you try to set me free of this world.

I run when you try to say time as come.

I run when you try to reach for my soul.

I RUN...
Because it is not time for me to be free like a pigeon
With no wings to fly.

I RUN...
Because it is not time yet for me to be free like a bear who
cannot lay an egg.

I RUN...
Because it is not my time...as I sit and watch like a owl
Watches for it enemies.

I RUN...
Because it is not my time! I run to find a safe place to hide
My soul away as I run, run, and run as a deer runs away from
A tiger with sharp teeth...I run out of my coma into my lifeless
Body as my breath spread throughout my lung, vein, my heart,
Into a living soul...I rise...
Because death is not coming for me today.

Don't go

Don't go and leave me alone…in this world with no wing to fly.

Don't go and leave me alone …in this world with no strength to try.

Don't go and leave me alone…in this world with no shoulder to cry.

Don't go and leave me alone…in this world with no fire to fry.

Don't go and leave me alone… don't go!

Death is calling

Death is calling you home today.

Death is calling out your name
and nobody can't hear but you.

Death is calling you to get ready.

Death is calling you to prepare your goodbye to your love ones.

Death is calling you to open all doors to your body.

Death is calling loud.

Death is calling louder.

But you cannot hear because time
Is going to fast… just when you think you have enough of time
Death just steps in and takes you away…

Farewell

Good night talk to you tomorrow

Good night talk to you tomorrow as the sun goes to rest.

Good night baby boy talk to you tomorrow as the birds fly to its nest.

Good night baby girl talk to you tomorrow as the student stays up to study for his test.

Good night to all talk to you tomorrow as I will be at my best.

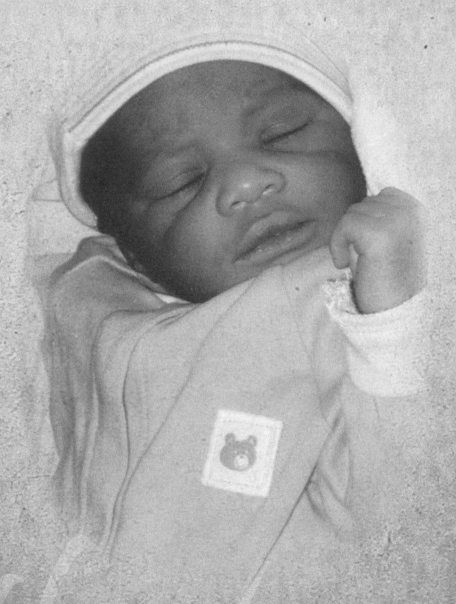

Good bye

This is my arm.
This is my hand.
This is my fingers… to wave good-bye to you

FAREWELL

Farewell to all.
Farewell to all as I wave good-bye to you
Standing on some blocks to be tall.
Farewell to all trying not to fall.

Go

I see you go.

You see me go.

We go to say good-bye.

Later

See you later
As I drink this glass of water.

Thanks

Thanks for your look.

Thanks for your hook.

Thanks for buying this and my next book.

Thanks…

The End

Printed in the United States
by Baker & Taylor Publisher Services